Why the C
Should Care About Housing

Graham Tomlin

Bishop of Kensington, President of St Mellitus College and Vice Chair of the Archbishop of Canterbury's Commission on Housing, Church and Community

Stephen Backhouse

Director of Tent Theology and Member of the Archbishop of Canterbury's Commission on Housing, Church and Community

GROVE BOOKS LIMITED

RIDLEY HALL RD CAMBRIDGE CB3 9HU

Contents

Acknowledgments

We would like to thank Archbishop Justin Welby for taking the lead in highlighting the need for a deeper theological understanding of housing, and to the members of his Commission on Housing, Church and Community for their feedback on earlier drafts. We are also grateful to all the theologians and housing practitioners who participated in several symposia on the theology of housing in September 2019 and November 2020, and who have helped immensely to inform and shape the ideas in this booklet.

First Impression January 2021
ISSN 1470-854X
ISBN 978 1 78827 149 3

1 Introduction

On 14 June 2017, a small fire started at the back of a fridge in a residential tower block in West London. Such a fire should have been contained by the design of the building to give time for it to be safely extinguished, yet as we all know, it soon spread across and up the whole of Grenfell Tower, killing 72 people, dramatically affecting the lives of many, and devastating a community. Those flames also spread to light up wider political issues in society, such as the gap between rich and poor, the value we place on social housing, gentrification and, of course, housing safety. They shone a light on what many had been talking of for years—what we call our housing crisis.

It is rare to find a day when the housing crisis does not hit the news in one way or another, whether related to unaffordable accommodation, a lack of social housing, poor quality living conditions or the persistent scandal of homelessness. Yet the issue goes back a long way before Grenfell. This is not the place to rehearse how we got to where we are today in housing—there are many books that tell that story well.[1] However, it is the place to think about what the church might have to say about it.

2 What Does Housing Have to Do with the Church?

There are many agencies with suggestions on how to solve the housing crisis. Charities, think tanks, experts in housing policy and academics all have their proposals to solve this complex problem. The church, however, is not just another social agency offering its solutions. Its primary loyalty, as Augustine insisted, is to the City of God, not to the City of this world. Its purpose is focused on the two great calls of the church—to worship the God and Father of Jesus Christ in the power of the Spirit and to bear witness to that same God.

That does not mean, however, that the church has no interest in the messy business of this world, such as the building, buying or renting of homes. In fact it is precisely in such a context that the church bears its witness. The church never bears witness to Christ in a vacuum—it always does it in the specific contexts of particular times and places.

The church never bears witness to Christ in a vacuum

We might think that housing has little to do with theology or the Christian gospel. After all, with a few notable exceptions, there has not been a great deal of theological analysis of housing or housing policy in the past.[2] Yet surely housing should matter to the church because it matters to all of us. Shelter is one of our most basic human needs, and most of us spend more time in our homes than we do anywhere else (and writing during the pandemic of 2020–21, most of us have spent more time at home this year than ever before). Unlike many other social or ethical issues, housing affects every one of us, because almost all of us have (or if we do not we should have) a place we call home. If God cares for all human life, then he cares about our homes because they matter to us.

Moreover, housing issues lie beneath so many of the pastoral and social problems that people face. So often, issues of social justice go back to housing, whether mental health issues exacerbated by poor home conditions, dysfunctional relationships aggravated by cramped and overcrowded housing, or social segregation due to differentiated land values. Many of the pastoral and social problems that churches and other social agencies have to tackle have a housing component. Rather than being involved in cure, churches can, if they choose, get involved upstream in prevention, by getting involved in the kind and quality of houses built that might prevent many of these problems in people's lives. If you visit areas of housing need, the same issues keep coming up. People will tell you of poor quality housing, the insecurity of living in tower blocks with flammable cladding, insecure tenancies, overcrowding, poor service from landlords and substandard accommodation. It is those voices that must be heard to help shape a theology of housing.

Behind all this, as we will soon see, the themes of houses, and the loss of home and land, are central to the story of salvation. Walter Brueggemann has argued that land and its use is one of the primary themes of the Bible.[3] We might go further and say specifically that the homes and houses that are built on land are also one of the key themes that run through the narrative arc of biblical history and theology.

Home in the Bible

The Bible tells a story of a journey from a God-provided home, of humanity then becoming 'homeless,' moving out into a hostile world, then of a long process of redemption which leads back home again, but to one that looks different from the first. Like the Prodigal Son, who leaves home only to return to it later in a way that reveals the full glorious character of the home he once left, the story takes the human race from its home with God in Eden, through expulsion from that home, to the place of return, to a final picture of God making his home with us. Throughout the story there is the recurrent theme of how this particularly affects the poor and suffering of the world.

In the New Testament, the word 'home' or 'house' or 'city' is used in a number of ways. In the gospels, it is often used in relation to the various places Jesus called home—Nazareth, Capernaum and Bethany. Yet another common use is for the world to come, as in:

> We have a building from God, a house not made with hands, eternal in the heavens. (2 Cor 5.1)
>
> For here we have no lasting city, but we are looking for the city that is to come. (Heb 13.14)
>
> In accordance with his promise, we wait for new heavens and a new earth, where righteousness is at home. (2 Pet 3.13)

These two themes capture the polarity of homes and housing in the Christian faith. On the one hand, home is a particular place—Nazareth, Nottingham or New York. Yet on the other hand, home is where God is, as he is our true home. When we are distant from God we are never truly at home, wherever we happen to be. And yet the two are related, because the same word 'home' (*oikos*) is used for both.

The final mention of home in the Bible brings these two perspectives together. It foresees the day when home is not found somewhere else, but when God makes his home with us.

> And I heard a loud voice from the throne saying, 'See, the home of God is among mortals. He will dwell with them; they will be his peoples, and God himself will be with them.' (Rev 21.3)

This is a picture of human destiny, both individual and corporate. It is to be at home with God our maker and redeemer. Our homes here are, therefore, to be signs, images, or anticipations of the home that is God's home—in the heavens, yet one day to take up residence here with us. So our homes and houses are viewed analogically—they are to be a picture, an analogy of our true home which is in God. Here is another reason why housing is a theological issue. If our homes and houses are in some measure to echo and give us a taste for our true home with God, then the quality and distribution of housing matters.

We are to value our homes, yet not to idolize them. This was the tension Israel lived with—that when they possessed land and forgot the God who gave it to them, they ended up losing that land. And yet their experience of exile opened up new possibilities of landedness that they could never have imagined before.

So our homes and houses are a gift and also a sign, perhaps even a sacramental sign, of the relationship of generous giver and grateful recipient into which we are invited. They are signs of the heavenly city that is our true home, and the goal of all human striving and longing. Yet in Christian understanding, signs and sacraments do not only point to the thing they signify, they also convey that very thing. So homes and houses do not merely act as signposts to our true home with God, they enable us to reach there too.

If our homes are in some way a sign of the future God has for us, then our theology of housing needs to take an eschatological shape—it needs to map onto the story of Scripture that leads towards its ultimate conclusion:

> I saw the Holy City, the new Jerusalem, coming down out of heaven from God, prepared as a bride beautifully dressed for her husband. And I heard a loud voice from the throne saying, 'Look! God's dwelling place is now among the people, and he will dwell with them. They will be his people, and God himself will be with them and be their God. He will wipe every tear from their eyes. There will be no more death or mourning or crying or pain, for the old order of things has passed away.' (Rev 21.2–4)

Christians, like many others, might get involved in homes and housing due to frustration at the injustice of the housing system, and that is a vital part of Christian motivation. However, even stronger than this, Christian engagement with housing is primarily driven and drawn by a vision of a future that beckons us and the whole of the created order, of creation as a place where God is at home with us and we are at home with God, a home which has no place for loss, isolation, neglect or brokenness, a vision of our true home. St Augustine famously prayed that 'Our hearts are restless until they find their rest in you,' which expresses that deep longing in the human heart for home, a place where we truly belong.

As Miroslav Volf puts it, the story of the gospel 'is an invitation to make our nested homes—family home, city-home, homeland, earth-home—reflect in some measure that coming home of God which completes creation.'

The primary question for the church is therefore not the obvious one—how to solve the problems in our housing market—but how can the church bear witness to the gospel of Jesus Christ in relation to the housing crisis? That is the crucial question this booklet seeks to answer.

The church is the community that God has called together to remind the rest of the world, through its words and actions, that one day he will 'make his home with us' (Rev 21.3). One of the ways the church can give people a taste of that kingdom of God here and now, bearing witness to God's past act of salvation and future promise, is to initiate projects and argue for policies that give people a taste of the true home we are promised one day. It is possible to tell the story of the gospel in bricks and mortar, in the creation of homes that can serve as an echo of our true home with God, but that is to get ahead of ourselves. The point is that the story of the gospel might have a lot more to say to us about housing than we think. And it may also be one of the arenas where the church has an opportunity to tell its story most clearly and visibly today.

The gospel may have a lot more to say about housing than we think

Tim Gorringe reminds us that 'All building expresses an ideology.'[4] So, for example, the current market-driven approach to housing so often expresses the idea that a home is a place to exclude other people, or a reward for success, or an asset to shield against the winds of change, something to put our trust, savings and wealth into. A Christian approach to housing, by contrast, is one that unashamedly embodies a vision of the story of the gospel. There are at least five pivotal moments in this story—creation, fall, redemption, the new community and the new creation. A five-fold theology of housing, church and community emerges from this story and takes shape as a witness to it insofar as it maps onto this story.

Creation: the need for Sustainability

In the beginning, the original creation was pronounced 'good' (Gen 1.31). It was given as a home for animal life of various kinds and ultimately, in time, the human race. The Garden of Eden is a picture of the divine provision of a space in which people can flourish and find fellowship with God, with other humans, and with the rest of the created order.

Two central themes emerge in the Bible's view of created land. Chris Wright points out that these are held together in two key themes of the psalms: 'The earth is the Lord's and all that is in it' (Ps 24.1) and 'The earth he has given to human beings' (Ps 115.16).[5] The earth, or the land, is both God's property and God's gift.

The witness of the prophets is that on the one hand, the specific promised land was never ultimately Israel's to own, as it remained God's possession, yet on the other hand it was given as a gift to Israel, as an inalienable expression and embodiment of God's generosity and love for his people. The gift of land was intended to bind the people to each other and to the God in whom they found their identity and well-being. Land, homes and houses were given not to create individual isolated enclaves, but to create a community in fellowship with God and each other.[6] With land comes moral obligation; land possession was dependent on observance of the Torah, otherwise the land will be lost. And that is, of course, exactly what happened in the exile, when the people of Israel lost their land and their home to the Assyrians and the Babylonians.

Homes were given to create a community in fellowship with God and each other

To translate this into terms familiar with housing and property, God is (as it were) the freeholder of land, which is then leased to humans as a gift. This, of course, radically relativizes human ownership of land. If God has all the rights and privileges of land ownership, then we are only ever the tenants and trustees of land. Moreover, with this gift of leased land, humanity is given responsibilities to 'work it and take care of it' (Gen 2.15 NIV). Responsibility for proper care and ongoing preservation of good land falls to the tenants. Land ownership brings with it not the license to exact as much produce or revenue from it as it will yield, but the responsibility to treat it well, and to ensure it is shared equitably.[7]

A housing policy that reflects the divine ownership and gifted nature of creation would therefore need to pay attention to the moral issues of the protection and sustainability of the land on which houses are built. Housing developments that are unsustainable, in the sense that they use too much of the earth's resources, are wasteful of energy or are out of sympathy with the natural environment and cannot bear witness to this part of the story.[8] We need to think of ourselves as stewards, not rulers of the natural world and of the properties we own or let out for rent. Housing policy needs to work with the grain of creation, to safeguard and not do violence to the earth God has given us.

Fallenness: the need for Safety

The second key moment in the biblical narrative is that of the fall. The human race, the very part of creation singled out to bear the divine image, to protect, nurture and develop the creation revolts against its maker and is consequently banished from the garden that was intended as their home. From this point on, their experience is one of violence (the killing of Abel in chapter 4), of nature as an enemy rather than a friend (the flood in chapters 6–9), and of confusion (the Tower of Babel in chapter 11). The security and safety of Eden is exchanged for the insecurity of a cold and hostile world. Left to its own devices, land and housing becomes concentrated in the hands of a few and divisions grow between rich and poor.

In the early days of Hebrew possession of the land, it seems to have been allocated to tribes, and within that to families—generationally-extended kinship groups that each possessed a portion of the land to sustain life and economic viability.[9] By the eighth century BC, a number of social changes, including a centralizing of state power, imposition of high levels of taxation, the growth of a wealthy class through the expansion of Solomon's empire, and battles with surrounding powers such as the Assyrians that decimated the peasantry, all led to a concentration of land and property in fewer hands, and the loss of land from the family kinship groups that originally farmed it.

The result was not just poverty, injustice and division, but ultimately exile and land loss. As the prophet Isaiah put it:

> Woe to you who add house to house
> and join field to field
> till no space is left
> and you live alone in the land.
> The Lord Almighty has declared in my hearing:
> 'Surely the great houses will become desolate,
> the fine mansions left without occupants.'
> Therefore my people will go into exile
> for lack of understanding;
> those of high rank will die of hunger
> and the common people will be parched with thirst. (Isa 5.8–10, 13)

When land use gets out of kilter, all kinds of social problems begin to rear their heads, and a society cannot last long when land is misused. The Old Testament was no stranger to a housing crisis.

Housing equity makes up around 60% of the UK's net worth. As a nation, we keep comparatively little in pensions or savings. For many people (though of course not all) their wealth is tied up in their home. Because in recent decades the price of houses has tended to rise inexorably, despite the odd fluctuation due to economic downturns, they remain one of the best investments on offer. As a result, houses have become investment vehicles, a place to tie up capital with a guaranteed return through rent, for example, selling on in due time, or something to leave to one's children. The downside of this is that housing can so often be seen as primarily a financial asset and other factors become secondary.

However, theologically speaking, rather than a financial asset, the gift of land and housing was intended, not only to meet a basic human need for shelter, but also to bind the people to each other and to God the creator. Land and home were given not to create private individual enclaves, but to create a community in fellowship with God and each other.

In Old Testament Israel, to deny people a share in the land and the sense of belonging that went with it was wrong, not because it infringed some modern principle of the sacredness of private property, but because being unable to share in the land meant being shut out from the community that enjoys together the grace and goodness of God. It meant denying people access to the life into which God had invited them—a life fully enjoying the blessing of God and neighbour, a full participation in the life God intended them to live. If the gift of God to people was land, then denying some people access to some form of trusteeship of land was to sever their relationship to God as the giver and to the covenant community that held that land.

Denying some people access to land was to sever their relationship to God

As Israel entered the promised land, to ensure the ongoing possibility of people sharing in the blessing of that land, the enactment of justice became vital. In this context Leviticus 25 becomes crucial, with its strong link between land possession and observance of the law:

> Follow my decrees and be careful to obey my laws, and you will live safely in the land. Then the land will yield its fruit, and you will eat your fill and live there in safety. (Lev 25.18–19)

Every 50 years there was to be a Jubilee year—a recalibration of ownership, with slaves being freed, and everyone returning to their ancestral lands. In between, land prices were to be related to the Jubilee principle, with prices dropping the nearer it came to the deadline year. There is proper scholarly debate as to whether the Jubilee year, as described in this passage, was ever enacted, but either way, it does indicate an ideal to which Israel aspired.

The basic principle of the Jubilee was not to prohibit land ownership or sale, or to impose absolute equality, but to protect land tenure by families so they were not allowed to drop out of the community into generational bondage. Those who ran up debts they could not pay would often have to sell land or even themselves into slavery. The Jubilee was a way to check that spiralling process into entrenched poverty. It also was designed to stop land being concentrated in a very few hands, as had happened in some of the surrounding nations where the kings owned all the land, with citizens as merely tenants, and as Isaiah 5 indicates, had begun to happen in Israel. The redemption of land, as Wright argues,

> ...was not provided so that an Israelite who, for whatever reason, failed to maintain his property should automatically and immediately have it restored to him, but that a person's descendants should not have to suffer in perpetuity the consequence of the economic collapse of his generation.[10]

If this expresses the inner logic of a biblical view of land, as God's possession, yet gifted in trust to us, to create a communal life in fellowship with God and each other, then it suggests a challenge to a view that allows a spiral of land value taking it out of the range of many and only accessible to the economically fortunate.

The doctrine of the fall narrates how this good world has been damaged, broken through the rejection of the creator by the creation, and is thus vulnerable and liable to decay. Unaided, it will descend into social and environmental disintegration. Home is an expression of ourselves, in that we choose the colours, décor, hang pictures, personalize the space. The destruction of home, such as what happened at Grenfell Tower, is therefore a kind of desecration, an invasion of the self that is much more significant than the loss of an office block or a railway station. As the Syrian architect Marwa al-Sabouni put it:

> Our homes don't just contain our life earnings, they stand for what we are. To destroy one's home should be taken as an equal crime to destroying one's soul.[11]

Housing that would bear witness to this part of the story of the gospel has, therefore, to pay attention to the need for safety and security against the threats to shared land and proper housing. Home is intended to be a safe place, where danger is kept at bay, a place of privacy where we know our own space will not be invaded against our will, and where we can feel secure from intrusion. Housing that testifies to the gospel needs to be safe space, offering shelter and security against damage and destruction. It needs to provide security against volatile market forces which create insecure owning or renting scenarios that lead to precarious lives. It needs to enable both financial affordability and personal security for both home owners and those who rent.

The Grenfell Tower story is one that vividly tells what happens when safety is relegated beneath other factors such as cost savings or even the demands of gentrification to raise the value of other surrounding properties.

This will, from time to time, as in the Jubilee principle, require specific intervention to prevent the (un)natural course of events whereby safe and secure housing is just the privilege of a few. Making housing safe, whether from fire, from rogue landlords or from the vagaries of the market, requires attention to issues of justice. The sight of people living in insecure tenancies or temporary accommodation, vulnerable to rent rises at the whim of landlords or developers, or to eviction at short notice, precisely reflects the insecurity reflected in the biblical story of the fall. Similarly, the way in which land continues to accrue more and more value over time, independent of any work done on it, so that landowners become increasingly wealthy while the houses on that land become unaffordable to anyone else, is a reflection, not of the divine will for land to bind people together, but of the brokenness of God's world.

On the political left there is an ideal of the perfectibility of people. On the political right there is an ideal of the perfectibility of markets. Christians are sceptical of both in this life. The market is not the enemy. But neither is it the sole solution. Here we find a mandate for specific intervention to ensure that, with regard to housing, markets reflect the vision of the kingdom of God, not the economic processes of a fallen world.

Incarnation: the need for Stability

The work of redemption of this broken world begins with the call of Abraham and the call of the people of Israel to the gift of living in a specific land provided by God. Christian faith later announces that into this broken world God has sent his Son, 'incarnate of the Virgin Mary,' dying for the sins of the world, rising again for the redemption of all things, with the promise of the Holy Spirit who forms and perfects us and all creation into maturity.

This part of the gospel story speaks of God entering the human story of soil and flesh. Far from some deist God who creates the world and then leaves it to run its course, God gets his hands dirty in the dust of the earth, as it were, by calling a 'wandering Aramaean,' by sending the prophets, and supremely in sending his Son, taking flesh, taking up residence in space and time. In Jesus Christ, 'the Word became flesh and blood, and moved into the neighbourhood' (John 1.14 *The Message*). God puts down roots in human flesh, history and places.

God puts down roots in human flesh, history and places

To bear witness to this part of the story, housing needs to provide the kind of stability that enables people to be rooted in places, staying in that same place for as long as they choose. Because of the incarnation, place and space matter. Stability means being able to put down roots, to feel we belong in a place and to a community over a period of time. Simone Weil, the French philosopher wrote, 'To be rooted is perhaps the most important and least recognized need of the human soul.'[12] When one of the Grenfell Tower survivors was asked why the hotel room in which he was placed after the fire did not feel like home, his reply was simple: 'Because it is not permanent.'

Part of sharing in the divine blessing, the invitation to life in fellowship with God, is the knowledge that we belong, both to God and to a wider community. Being constantly uprooted from home denies us the capacity to belong, to develop long-term relationships that can bring support during difficult times and that help mould us into mature human beings. Stability in a physical place and community that enables us to put down roots is essential for the kind of formation to maturity that is crucial for human flourishing.

At the most basic level, we build houses for shelter. We need a place that can protect us from the elements of rain, sun or wind. Yet there is much more to a home than this. Wendell Berry asks the provocative question, *What Are People For?*[13] The Christian answer to that question, taking our cue from Jesus when asked almost the same question, must be that we are here to love God and to love our neighbour.

Yet that is not something that comes naturally to us. It might come naturally to love and take care of ourselves, but not necessarily to love and take care of our neighbour as ourselves. We have to learn it. And home is one of the key places that we learn to do this. Homes are places where we grow towards maturity, towards the goal of our earthly journey, which is to be with the God who is both our origin and our goal.

Humans are made to grow to maturity, which in Christian understanding means growth in love for God (which involves *gratitude* for all we have been given) and neighbour (which means *generosity* towards those placed right next to us). This is what mature humanity looks like. We therefore need contexts in which such formation happens. The primary place in which such formation happens, at least in early years, is family, and there is a particularly strong link between family, home and housing in the Bible, particularly in the Hebrew Scriptures.

The Book of Deuteronomy invites the people of God to study the laws of God, and in particular to 'recite them to your children and talk about them when you are at home and when you are away, when you lie down and when you rise' (Deut 6.7, see also 11.10). The brief glimpses we get of Jesus as a child at home refer to his growth in maturity: '...they returned to Galilee, to their home town of Nazareth. The child grew and became strong, filled with wisdom; and the favour of God was upon him' (Luke 2.39–40). Elsewhere in the New Testament, the family home is presented as a place of formation and growth: '"Honour your father and mother"—which is the first commandment with a promise—"so that it may go well with you and that you may enjoy long life on the earth...Fathers, do not exasperate your children; instead, bring them up in the training and instruction of the Lord"' (Eph 6.1–4).

In the earliest period of the church, homes were routinely used as the venue for church life (for example, 1 Cor 16.19; Col 4.15; Phile 2). Home was a place for worship and communal life, alongside more formal settings for gathering: 'Every day they continued to meet together in the temple courts. They broke bread in their homes and ate together with glad and sincere hearts' (Acts 2.46). Home was a place of instruction, or formation, where in the context of family and wider friendships and relationships, both children and adults learnt wisdom and grew into maturity, bearing in mind that households in biblical times were much wider and more extensive than the nuclear family of today.

Homes and houses are the primary contexts in which we grow into maturity

Homes and houses are one of the primary contexts in which we grow into maturity. This is particularly true for children but it is also true for adults as well. Those who live together are necessarily shaped by the experience of having to live alongside and manage the joys and tensions of close proximity with others. Even those who live alone can and do find home a place of formation, through such regular practices as reading, watching TV, reflecting on life experiences, or welcoming others into their homes.

That is why we need stable housing—so we can put down roots in a place and a community and be formed by that community into maturity.

The New Community: the need for Sociability

The fourth moment in the arc of the biblical narrative comes with Pentecost—the sending of the Spirit and the forming of a new community—the church.

At the heart of the Christian gospel is welcome into fellowship, to communion with God and with the people that he gathers. In creation we are provided with and welcomed into a world which is not ours, and we are urged to delight in it. Throughout the Hebrew Scriptures, the invitation of God is issued to his people to sit and eat with him:

> Everyone who thirsts,
> come to the waters;
> and you that have no money,
> come, buy and eat!
> Come, buy wine and milk
> without money and without price. (Isa 55.1)

In Holy Comunion, the invitation to sit and eat at the table of God is given physical form. The vision of the new Jerusalem concludes with the same invitation: 'The Spirit and the bride say, "Come!" And let the one who hears say, "Come!" Let the one who is thirsty come; and let the one who wishes take the free gift of the water of life' (Rev 22.17).

Hospitality creates sociability. It is something we receive. It is also something we are called to give. David Walker, the Bishop of Manchester, tells the story of an immigrant to the UK, who had been conscious of being a guest of his adopted nation for many years. On moving into his own home for the first time he remarked on how, for the first time, this enabled him to be host, not just guest, in a place that was now his own.[14] To be in a position to offer hospitality confers dignity on a person as imaging God in his own generosity.

The NT Greek word for hospitality is *philoxenia*—literally 'love of the stranger'—and the theme is prominent in the list of characteristics which mark out a Christian view of home. Instructions to exhibit hospitality abound, for example:

> Contribute to the needs of the saints; extend hospitality to strangers. (Rom 12.13)
>
> Be hospitable to one another without complaining. (1 Pet 4.9)
>
> Do not neglect to show hospitality to strangers, for by doing that some have entertained angels without knowing it. (Heb 13.2)

The size and role of households has, of course, changed significantly since NT times. Most households are now smaller and the hospitality industry is much more developed. Now, when staying in an unfamiliar town, we use hotels and restaurants, rather than relying on being taken into a local home. Showing hospitality to visitors is less of a cultural expectation than it was in biblical times.[15] Yet the practice remains, perhaps in a different shape, but as a central aspect of the way a home is to be used in Christian understanding, because hospitality creates community, and living in community is part of the divine will for human life.

Public space needs to be sociable, to create a sense of society. And to do this it needs to be generous. Marwa al-Sabouni, in her evocative description of the architecture of her home city of Homs, later destroyed in the Syrian conflict, speaks about older Syrian cities as 'generous cities' that offered free water fountains, benches and shady trees in open spaces during hot days. Public space was attractive and given priority in the design of housing development.[16] Housing that reflects God's welcome to us needs to provide space for hospitality and welcome. Overcrowded accommodation makes welcoming the neighbour or stranger difficult. Similarly, housing designed to build miniature castles, isolated enclaves that essentially shut out the neighbour and are incapable of building community cannot bear witness to the gospel of welcome.

A home is not neutral community space. There is a need for such communal space in neighbourhoods. Yet, homes and houses are also private spaces into which friends, neighbours and even strangers can be invited on occasion and when chosen by the host. If we are shaped and formed by interaction with others, then inviting others into our own personal and private space will be one way in which we allow ourselves to be formed by others and invite them to be formed by us. It will also create a broader sense of community and welcome within a particular neighbourhood once this becomes normal practice. A Christian view of housing must include the possibility for anyone to act as host in their own home, however small or limited that might be.

Resurrection: the need for Satisfaction

The culmination of the story of Jesus is his resurrection. The climax of the Bible is the resurrection of the world into a new creation, a vision of the earth restored, purged of suffering, misery and injustice, of the triumph of life and love. The vision of Revelation 21, with a city of jewels, with streets of gold and vibrant colour, is meant to evoke a sense of wonder at the beauty of this vision: 'It has the glory of God and a radiance like a very rare jewel, like jasper, clear as crystal' (Rev 21.11). This is no grey, colourless place, a brutalist concrete prison, but a city that shines with splendour. It is a place of streets, buildings, walls, gates and measuring sticks. In other words, it is a place where human artifice, ingenuity and technology is used, not to deny life or to dull the senses, but to create beauty, to allow in the light of God's glory, to create a space for human and other life to find joy. It is also a place where dishonesty, lack of courage, the idolatry of an exclusive focus on profit and the taking of human life are all excluded (Rev 21.8). These aspects of our common experience, which cause so much damage to social life, especially in housing, will all be banished from the City of God.

People flourish and mature well in spaces that they enjoy

People flourish and mature well in spaces that they enjoy and which stimulate wonder and pleasure. Dull, harsh and unforgiving built environments do not encourage investment in those places, nor the communities they contain—a brutal environment brutalizes people. To take pleasure in our environment is to take pride in it, to want to preserve and make it stable, to ensure its sustainability and longevity. Tim Gorringe writes about an 'aesthetics of creation, responding sympathetically to the environment, rather than trying to "tame" it.'[17]

The beauty of the new Jerusalem is tied up with what lies at its centre—the fact that God dwells with mortals. It is lit not by the sun, but by the glory of God. What makes the city beautiful is not just its stones, but its relationships. Hence Gorringe also writes of the 'aesthetics of community,' and points to the conditions that can make the built environment beautiful, namely: respect for the natural created environment; exuding life; respect for the past; communal spaces and buildings; caring for the poor and their living conditions.[18]

Housing needs to satisfy us. Our homes need to be places we enjoy living in, we delight to come home to, just as we long to come home to our true destination in the new Jerusalem. Attention to the aesthetic quality of accommodation will be important for a Christian vision of housing that can be a sign of the new creation. It will also be significant for the aspect of home as a place of formation as well. The beauty or otherwise of the built environment has a significant impact on mental health and hence well-being.[19] We shrink in places of drabness, but flourish and are able to grow in places of beauty and life.

3 The Necessity of Sacrifice

So we have discovered that the five aspects of the biblical narrative lead us to these five core values for a Christian vision of housing. Homes that echo the coming kingdom of God, that give a taste of the coming home that we are promised at the end of the story of salvation will be *sustainable, safe, stable, sociable* and *satisfying*.

There is, however, one more aspect that stands apart from the rest. It is not so much a descriptor of good housing as such, but a value that arises from the heart of the gospel, without which our housing crisis will never be solved. It is the centrality of sacrifice.

The work of redemption involves not just the Word becoming flesh, but that flesh being torn and broken on the cross, atoning for the sins of the world, bringing forgiveness, reconciliation of a divided humanity (Eph 2.16) and then raised to the right hand of God to bring about the ultimate healing of the brokenness of the world. Jesus speaks of his body as a building—a temple that is destroyed and then raised again (John 2.21). The healing of a broken world comes about not through an exercise of force or violence, but through sacrificial love. The love of God is seen most clearly in the sacrificial death of Christ, and there is no love without sacrifice.

The healing of a broken world comes about through sacrificial love

The eschatological vision that drives Christian involvement with housing cannot be achieved without a sense of sacrifice—the sacrifice of privilege, of power, and potential profits that could be made. For example, making housing secure for people involves supplying truly affordable housing, which will in turn involve developers and landowners (including the church) to accept less immediate profit than they might otherwise get for their land, putting the needs of others (and the poorest in particular) above the maximization of short-term financial gain. Keeping rents within the means of tenants will involve a willingness on behalf of landlords not just to accept what the market will offer, but to retain rents at a level that relates to what tenants can pay. Keeping houses and homes safe will involve sacrifice, investing time, money and energy to ensure the safety of our neighbours, especially in social housing. The true test of compassion is whether we are willing to sacrifice our own interests for the interests of others as Christ did, especially for those at the receiving end of housing injustice (Phil 2.4–5). Justice is never achieved without it.

To take one example, a common factor whenever a new housing development is proposed, particularly one that involves social housing, is resistance—not in my back yard! Now, there may be plenty of good reasons to be a NIMBY. Precisely none of them are open to followers of the way of Jesus.

4 The Temptation of NIMBYism

There are a number of variations that 'Not in my backyard' takes. Ultimately, however, the core principle boils down to the moral right of people to protect and preserve their patch of land, because it is their patch of land. As it stands, this is a knockdown argument in favour of NIMBYism. Who can protest against the moral right of someone to clutch tightly to what is rightfully theirs, when it is indeed rightfully theirs? As with much else in Western liberal democracy, the conversations around NIMBYism are negotiations about the hierarchy of rights. The rights of landowners or long-term residents are contrasted with the rights of newcomers who need to live somewhere, or rival property owners who wish to develop their land. A success for the NIMBY is legal, public and cultural validation that their rights trump that of their rivals. In the hierarchy of rights, NIMBYs own the space, and everyone else must adapt or move on.

This is all well and good for most backyards of the land. But it poses a problem for people who find themselves to be responsible for Christian backyards. This is because the core principle for followers of the way of Jesus is that they are not to clutch tightly to what is rightfully theirs, even when it is indeed rightfully theirs. To paraphrase Matt 10.25–26, 'You know those people who do not fear God and lord their power over others? Do not be like them.' The conversation for the follower of the way of Christ does not begin or end with locating their position in the hierarchy of rights. Their mission in this world is not connected to their rights at all. Time and time again, Jesus asks his followers to adopt attitudes and actions of open-handedness towards being wronged even when (especially when!) the knockdown argument of what is right falls in their favour.

Followers of Jesus are not to clutch tightly to what is rightfully theirs

A litany of examples can be found in the Sermon on the Mount. Turning the other cheek, going the extra mile, and giving a coat as well when sued for a cloak are all instances of the kind of orientation Jesus people had towards their rightful claim over the stuff of life. A person being struck is allowed to strike back—indeed, they should. Roman soldiers were entitled to commandeer someone to carry their pack one mile; a person could drop the pack after one mile and not a court in the land would find against them. Jewish law does not allow for someone to be completely impoverished by losing a case; they are legally, morally and ethically entitled to keep their clothes. And yet Jesus suggests another way. At every turn, Jesus is asking his people not to limit their moral horizon at what is rightfully due to them.

The teaching is not confined to theoretical examples from a sermon. In telling the whole story of Jesus, the gospels portray what is sometimes called a cruciform life. Jesus' lived example is of someone who is patently innocent of all the charges against him. By their own logic, inherited traditions, priestly laws and Roman legal systems should find him in the right, yet he allows these things to kill him anyway. 'I lay my life down of my own accord and I have authority to take it up again' (John 10.18). The story, of course, does not end with death. The resurrection recommends the way of Jesus' life to all creation. The resurrection of Jesus is not portrayed in the New Testament as an isolated magic trick. It is the culmination of the cruciform life, an affirmation of the open-handedness Jesus had towards his own entitlements. In the Book of Acts it was the resurrected cruciform life which inspired Paul to move towards Rome and persecution despite multiple times of being found innocent. It was this which prompted Barnabas to sell his land, and Lydia, the wealthy merchant of purple cloth, to open her home to poor and marginal followers of the Way. It was the resurrected cruciform life which led the earliest church not to organize themselves around accumulation of power and the hierarchy of rights. Instead, mutual submission ('everyone submit one to another,' Eph 5.21), self-sacrifice ('lay down your lives,' 1 John 3.16), and subverted privilege ('the parts considered less honourable we treat with special honour,' 1 Cor 12.23) abound.

The earliest followers of Jesus followed the cruciform way of their master

The earliest followers of Jesus had their rights and knew their laws. They recognized the privilege and responsibility that comes from inherited wealth and position. They owned buildings and land. Many of them had backyards. Then, as now, NIMBYism was a valid option. Yet at each and every turn, these people followed the cruciform way of their master, who invites his people to consider neighbours and enemies better than themselves, not to be anxious about anything, and not to clutch tightly to what is rightfully ours, even when it is indeed rightfully ours.

Much as we might like to think the housing crisis can be solved without pain, this is not true. It is already causing pain and suffering to many. It can only be solved by sharing that pain among all parties involved in a broken system. Yet the Christian gospel says that through and after the cross comes resurrection. The path to salvation lies through, not around, sacrifice. The question is whether we are content to allow that pain to continue to be borne by those who have little voice and power, or whether all parties who are involved in the complexities of the housing system (including the church!) will bear their share of sacrifice in order to ensure a better future for all. And this will always involve an element of risk, which is at the heart of faith and Christian obedience. Yet as insecure, sinful humans, even as Christians, we tend to be averse to risk.

The Inevitability of Risk

The early Christians often spoke of 'powers and principalities'. It is from their open-handed attitude towards these things that we can derive our approach to risk when it comes to institutions for which we are responsible. Despite popular (and unpopular) opinion, 'powers and principalities' are not merely the realm of faith healers and exorcists. Sometimes in the New Testament they refer to demons and angels. But most of the time these words and concepts are used to refer to social and political institutions: government, traditional holidays, families, measurements of distance and time, common sense and the rule of law are all described using power and principality language. The common thread linking spiritual beings with human institutions is that a principality is a faceless force which influences our life. Furthermore, it is a phenomenon which had a creator and an original purpose.

A principality is a faceless force which influences our life

A principality is angelic when it accepts its created nature and purpose. It is demonic when it bursts its bounds, claims too much and acts like a self-made little god. Following Jesus, who reminded the Pharisees that the Sabbath was made for humans and not humans for the Sabbath, the early Christian response to powers that burst their bounds was to put them back in the box. 'For by him all things were created: things in heaven and on earth, visible and invisible, whether principalities or powers or rulers or authorities; all things were created by him and for him' (Col 1.16). The letter to the Colossians is a good example of this way of thinking, using powers and principalities language to describe the range of forces that were set against the way of Jesus. Inherited morality, national allegiance, religious observations, legal demands, the empire of Rome, and yes, even spiritual creatures, are all seen as powers which were exposed as grasping for dominance. 'And having disarmed the powers and authorities, he made a public spectacle of them, triumphing over them by the cross' (Col 2.15).

The story of the powers gone right is the story of humans arranging themselves in ways that lead to the right worship of God and *shalom*—peaceful flourishing amongst all people. The story of powers gone wrong is the story of structures, organizations and inherited forms of life that resist having their supremacy challenged, placing the good of the institution above that of the people it was created for. Principalities that resist reformation dig their heels in, entrenching themselves in their power and keeping their resources out of circulation. 'You know that the rulers of the Gentiles lord it over them, and their high officials exercise authority over them. Not so with you. Instead, whoever wants to become great among you must be your servant' (Matt 20.25). The earliest followers were highly aware of the tendency for man-made institutions to burst their bounds and claim too much. The Christian people charged with responsibility for the structures and resources they had inherited thus took a stance that was open to risk. They did not see themselves primarily as preserving or prolonging their institutions (families, religious organizations, economic networks, national groups). Instead they were open-handed with these things, willing to give away accumulated power or restructure if that is what best served people according to the way of Jesus. A case in point can be found in Acts 6 where the inherited traditional responsibility to care for one's own poor was deliberately dismantled by the appointment of Stephen and the other deacons to make sure that resources were distributed, and Greek widows flourished.

Likewise, the common sense and conservative ordering of the traditional family roles were upended by the Christian imagination. Where Romans naturally assumed the rightful ordering of the family hierarchy, with everyone ranged under the man in decreasing levels of importance and personal agency, texts such as Ephesians and 1 Peter risk the institution of family and hierarchical power by insisting that an attitude of submission was for everyone. 'Servants submit to your masters...Masters do likewise.' The concrete result of the effect of this teaching can be seen in the early church practice where everyone 'considers others as more important than themselves' (Phil 2). The Christian ethic was not confided to individual lives. They knew that following the way of Jesus is corporate, organized and instituted, baked into the household codes and rules of life that can be found in multiple places throughout the New Testament. Organized obedience to the way of Jesus that eschews accumulated power is spiritual warfare. It is, for example, the politically radically practice of mutual submission in Ephesians 5 which forms the bedrock of the struggle against powers and principalities in Ephesians 6.

Organized obedience to the way of Jesus is spiritual warfare

The housing crisis will not be solved without taking big risks. Yet it is one thing for individuals to risk their own resources for personal gain, and quite another when what is being risked is the inherited legacy of institutional, shared and organized public goods. Housing is not a private matter. The issue of housing takes in the whole gamut of interconnected human life: economics, business structures, relational networks, institutions, land management, historical legacy, inherited traditions and other forms of social and political organzation.

When we examine the housing crisis, various institutions come under the spotlight when it comes to the way their resources are—or are not—being used to promote a just and good approaching to housing. The hope is that organizations made up of people following the way of Jesus will embrace risk, even (especially!) when it means reforming their institutions and using their inherited resources to serve people well. An aversion to risk can be angelic when it takes the form of good stewardship: using the resources well that one has inherited and leaving them to the next generation better than you received them. But aversion to risk in this sense is only good if the institution we are stewarding is doing what it should do and serving the people it should serve. An aversion to risk becomes diabolical when it preserves the institution because it is the institution. Here, inherited resources or forms of life take precedence over the flourishing of our neighbours. This is especially a problem for followers of Jesus, because the only point of any of our institutions is to lead to the flourishing of our neighbours. Love God and love your neighbour. There is no greater commandment. The housing crisis will not br resolved without sacrifice. And sacrifice always involved the risk that it might not be worth it. but it is a risk we have to take, and one that we hope the church will be first in line to take.

5

Conclusion

How can the church bear witness to the gospel of Christ in the arena of housing? The Church of England in particular is both a major landowner and also has a voice in public policy through its established status in society. The Church can bear its witness to the gospel by building houses and housing developments that explicitly seek to display the elements we have seen emerging from the narrative arc of Scripture—housing that is sustainable, safe, stable, sociable and satisfying. It also does it by leading by example in the realm of being willing to make sacrifices and take risks when it comes to the use and sale of land, for the sake of those who live in its houses or on its land. It can also argue for such values to permeate public housing policy, in such a way that we see ourselves as stewards rather than controllers of the earth, alert to the call of justice, seeking spaces for human formation into maturity, exhibiting a generosity of space and place and housing that brings delight and joy, because that is what we were made for.

Appendix: Further Reading

M al-Sabouni, *The Battle for Home* (London: Thames and Hudson, 2016)

W Berry, *What are People For? Essays by Wendell Berry* (New York: North Point Press, 1990)

J Boughton, *Municipal Dreams: The Rise and Fall of Council Housing* (London: Verso, 2018)

W Brueggemann, *The Land: Place as Promise and Challenge in Biblical Faith* (Minneapolis, MN: Fortress, 2002)

D Dorling, *All That is Solid: How the Great Housing Disaster Defines our Times and What We Can Do About It* (London: Penguin, 2015)

A Francis, *Foxes Have Holes: Christian Reflections on Britain's Housing Need* (London: Ekklesia, 2016)

T J Gorringe, *A Theology of the Built Environment: Justice, Empowerment, Redemption* (Cambridge University Press, 2002)

W Heaven, 'What building beautiful can do for mental health' in J Airey, *Building Beautiful*, Policy Exchange: https://policyexchange.org.uk/publication/building-beautiful/ pp 112–117.

C Pohl, *Making Room: Recovering Hospitality as a Christian Tradition* (Grand Rapids, MI: Eerdmans, 1999)

R Sennett, *Building and Dwelling: Ethics for the City* (London: Allen Lane, 2018)

G Tomlin and M Brown (eds), *Coming Home: A Theology of Housing* (London: Church House Publishing, 2020)

S Weil, *The Need for Roots* (London: Routledge, 2002)

C J H Wright, *God's People in God's Land: Family, Land and Property in the Old Testament* (Carlisle: Paternoster, 1990)

Notes

1 See, for example, A Francis, *Foxes Have Holes: Christian Reflections on Britain's Housing Need* (London: Ekklesia, 2016). D Dorling, *All That is Solid: How the Great Housing Disaster Defines our Times and What We Can Do About It* (London: Penguin, 2015). J Boughton, *Municipal Dreams: The Rise and Fall of Council Housing* (London: Verso, 2018).

2 For such examples, see T J Gorringe, *A Theology of the Built Environment: Justice, Empowerment, Redemption* (Cambridge University Press, 2002) and, more recently, G Tomlin and M Brown (eds), *Coming Home: A Theology of Housing* (London: Church House Publishing, 2020).

3 W Brueggemann, *The Land: Place as Promise and Challenge in Biblical Faith* (Minneapolis, MN: Fortress, 2002).

4 T J Gorringe, *A Theology of the Built Environment: Justice, Empowerment, Redemption* (Cambridge University Press, 2002).

5 C J H Wright, *God's People in God's Land: Family, Land and Property in the Old Testament* (Carlisle: Paternoster, 1990) p 116.

6 *ibid*, p 135ff.

7 For expansion of this point, see W *Brueggemann, The Land: Place as Promise and Challenge in Biblical Faith, op cit*, pp 56–62.

8 This point is made strongly in T J Gorringe, *A Theology of the Built Environment, op cit*, chapter 9.

9 See C J H Wright, *God's People in God's Land, op cit*, chapter 2.

10 *ibid*, p 124.

11 M al-Sabouni, *The Battle for Home* (London: Thames and Hudson, 2016) p 57.

12 S Weil, *The Need for Roots* (London: Routledge, 2002) p 43.

13 W Berry, *What Are People For? Essays by Wendell Berry* (New York: North Point Press, 1990).

14 A Francis, *Foxes Have Holes, op cit*, p 9.

15 See C Pohl, *Making Room: Recovering Hospitality as a Christian Tradition* (Grand Rapids, MI: Eerdmans, 1999) for an excellent discussion of the significance of hospitality in Christian history and activity. Richard Sennett remarks on the shift in the nineteenth century from public space in cities as a place where you would expect to meet and interact with strangers, to one where we expect to be left alone. R Sennett, *Building and Dwelling: Ethics for the City* (London: Allen Lane, 2018) p 27f.

16 M al-Sabouni, *The Battle for Home, op cit*, chapter 3.

17 T J Gorringe, *A Theology of the Built Environment, op cit*, p 208.

18 *ibid*, pp 217–220.

19 See W Heaven, 'What building beautiful can do for mental health' in J Airey, *Building Beautiful*, Policy Exchange: https://policyexchange.org.uk/publication/building-beautiful/ pp 112–117.